Writings from The Soul

PETER LEBUHN

 www.trafford.com
North America & international
toll-free: 1 888 232 4444 (USA & Canada)
fax: 812 355 4082

Peter LeBuhn(2-21-64)

GROWING UP IN THE LATE 1960'S AND 1970'S, MY MUSICAL AND POETIC INFLUENCES WERE VAN MORRISON THE BEATLES AND THE MAMAS AND THE PAPAS. NOW, A LOCAL WRITER IN THE PHILADELPHIA AREA. MANY WORDS THAT ARE WRITTEN AND SPOKEN ARE FROM REAL LIFE AND FEELING. THIS IS WHAT I ATTEMPT TO CONVEY TO THE READER AS I WRITE, TO PULL THE READER INTO THE EXPERIENCE AS I WRITE. MANY OF MY WRITINGS ARE SPIRTUAL AND ROMANTIC IN NATURE. THEY ARE ALL WRITTEN FROM THE HEART. MY WAY OF SHARING WITH ALL OF YOU WHO I AM.

IF YOU WOULD LIKE TO REACH ME MY BUSINESS PAGE IS MY POETRY PAGE IS LEBUHNWRITINGS. COM WRITING POETRY SINCE 1983, I HAVE BEEN ABLE TO EXPRESS MY EMOTIONS FROM SPIRTUAL, ROMANTIC, EXOTIC AND TIGER POEMS THAT I WROTE FOR A SAVE THE TIGER CAMPAIGN IN NEPAL FOR ARCHANA SHRESTA, A GOOD FRIEND.

ALL OF THESE WRITINGS CAME FROM MY HEART THEY ARE TRULY "POEMS FROM THE HEART"

Peter Benjamin Le Buhn

I Dedicate this book to all lovers of the written word and
poetry and I hope these words speak to your life

A Second Chance

a second chance
to dance
to live...to sing...to be thankful
to give

set apart this opulent opportunity
not for myself
fot i am put on the shelf
a second chance to serve and not swerve

with a narrow faith
ne'er to swerve
once fallen...broken wings
understanding how to serve my king

all of my heart
all of my mind
all of my soul

A SECOND CHANCE
A SECOND CHANCE

Peter LeBuhn

Beacon Of Light

you are my beacon of light
illumination lights thy path
trail walked
course taken

UNKNOWN
my heart IS
filled with your love
treasure for creation
your teachings are my nation
your ways my incarnation

beacon of light
there is no fright
the darkness made bright

one scripture...one christ
one word...one GOD
ONE GLORY the
five solar forever
ring true

Peter LeBuhn

Butterfly

like a butterfly
you rest on the evening star
...where you are resting afar
the song which holds our spirit kindred
live from day to night

Many struggles...
Many tears....
,,,, Many embraces

the joy of something grand
a cultivated harmonious friendship
...with no limits
...you are a friend without blemish
...you stole my heart

making my stand
...these dreams
...these thoughts of you
unexplained
...what say you of me?

my precious butterfly
don't fly far
...don't fly far

Peter LeBuhn

China Rose

my china rose
in the white of the snow
a glimpse of you is caught
walking like a china rose

i testify
to the heights of the sky
you i cannot let fly by

this china rose
the way she looks at thee
with a certain prose
my heart glows

her smile has made it worthwhile
my china rose
my china rose

Peter LeBuhn

Court Of Love

an anniversary song
answers in a game of questions
after the sensation
the midnight hour

increases thy power
...thy love higher from above
coming before thee
NAKED...BARE...RAW

in your court of love
...found guilty
you sentence thee
to a lifetime of passion

by the river we go
a care
ne'er to take
our love we partake
an anniversary song will be sung
forever will be sung

Peter LeBuhn

Duece Game

is it advantage in
or advantage out
or deuce
many questions surround my heart.

unsure of what has been entered into
knowing what is seen
it is good and blessed
director we will take will see

many questions
remain unasked
dancing delicately
in and out of conversations

in time you will know and grow.
heart is softening.
no many questions to be asked
soon will no longer remain

it will be a good duece game-equal partnership.

Peter LeBuhn

Electrical Storm

living a life that is sunny
walking around
i am happy
now feeling funny

what is going on
what is happening
an electrical storm
a party is going on in my brain
one that i can't explain

don't like this party
don't want to be here
living in fear
that is no way to live

living with a light on my heart
thy life from here will make my start
a start of sharing and caring

Peter LeBuhn

Exploring A Mystery

Exploring a mystery
brings the warmth of sun to my heart
when we apart
i think of you in blissful mystery
for the rest of my days

your hair unfurled
in golden locks of disarray
as the sun shines upon you

your eyes invite me
as we frolic near the stream
nearer you come to thee

beaming
shining
beauty inviting

binding you may be
i cannot help but be hypnotized
hypnotized by your captive beauty
my heart pounds like a drum
happiness has entered my life

Peter LeBuhn

Expressionless Page

the expressionless page
to an expressionless page
my pen takes action
the words of my heart flow with passion

a story is being written
a drama
a comedy
a tragedy (i hope not)

in my heart
i know what is real and true
every moment
every second

the pen makes a new entry
the page has new meaning and feeling
history is being made
where my pen takes thee
the futureis yet to be seen

Peter LeBuhn

Grace and Honor

to you i give grace
to you i give honor
you are the One
...That has allowed thee to save face

trials and turmoils
troubles and boils
you are there
in all of this universe
there is no compare

the one true
you make my soul anew

to you true
obedience is mine
i am yours
your ways i climb

Peter LeBuhn

Greatness

greatness falls upon thee
rain showers on a stormy day.
storms...weatherd
trials...sustained

lives touched
life becomes stronger
my testimony reaches further
with each individual.

this greatness is a gift from the father
he gave me the talents'
he gave me the water and clay to nuture and mold them

the seeds have grown
to many in his name
thank you father
for this humble greatness
thank you father

Peter LeBuhn

Harvest Phantasy

the day is dark...
rainy...and whet
with her life is illuminating and warm

as we frolic in the rain
with all the passion and vigor
that our hearts can generate
arms wrapped with a tender embrace

the rain has ceased
the sun has risen
all the colors of the rainbow are upon us
as we lay in a mountain full of colorful leaves

looking at her
knowing she is joyful
because of the smile in her wyes
and the smile on her face

Peter LeBuhn

Hearts Uncharted

smiling to thee from afar
name...it is unknown
heart warms to a roaring flame
drumbeats become louder by the second.

still...not a sound
inviting me to YOUR WORLD
a world of the unknown
many pages will be written on blank pages

the course of the story is uncharted
no one else has to read our book
not even us

finding out who you are
as for the pages
the first entry is you

Peter LeBuhn

Hold On

the moon shines bright
stars overlook above
a clear night
separated afar

do you think of thee
does your heart beat for me
hold on...hold on tight
to the one you love

times of trial abound us
temptations around
hold on
hold on tight

you must believe what you have is true
let's keep it simple
what we have will grow day by day

second by second
minute by minute
hour by hour
day by day

week by week
month by month
year by year
hold on
hold

Peter LeBuhn

In The Groove of The Night

in the groove of the night
free of fright
the moon shines bright
like a spy

the tide roars in
expectation about to begin
watching all of this happen

in the groove of the night
the portal of passion found
not paying attention to a sound

you lost in me
i in you

in the groove of the night
passion has taken flight

Peter LeBuhn

In The Hush Calm of The Twilight

in the hush calm of the twilight
when day becomes night
no doubt moonlight to trespass
on our eve
envisioning the glisten in your eyes
as we lay stylishly nude

performing love sonnets
the sheet music of hearts...of the charts
delicate and tender
intrigue of a love story surrounds the melody of thy heart
flavor of stimulation, excitation, arousal
wrapped in your arms

engrossing to my clutches
candles shine their flame blazing on our passions
the sweet scent of perfume
drives my desire higher

the expression in your eyes
the sensation of your succulent thighs before thee

whispering poetry and passion to you
you lost in my body i am lost in yours
lost in erotic fashion
thy body comes alive

your the heat of my desire
passions into action
your flavor...i belabor

in the hush calm of the twilight
in the hush calm of the twilight

Peter LeBuhn

In Your Eyes

in your eyes
the future is seen
in your eyes
the road is clear and clean

in your eyes
there is happiness and joy
in your heart
more love to give

ne'er to depart
in your heart
the greater your reward

in your hands
you take mine
in your hands
you take mine

in your eyes
in your eyes

Peter LeBuhn

Invincible Tiger

unlimited power
the tiger watches over us
ultimate protection and care
evil not to enter

not even to dare
the mighty tiger
ever knowing
ever watching
invisible is she

...her family
keeping her family and pride intact
so strong the possession attract
kingly...queenly

sovereign grace
over their place
the mighty tiger
invincible
forever...shall reign

Peter LeBuhn

Key To Your Heart

let me unlock the key
to your heart
so i can unlock the secret chambers of love...
FOREVER

Peter LeBuhn

Magic of Love in The Moonlight

from a distance seeing thee
dressed in cool white
sweet curves of thy body shine through
our meeting...long last...happenstance

our eyes
how they glisten
outlined against the shimmering sands
closer to each other

stars shining in a myriad
twinkling lights celebrating in harmony with joy
feeling love between us

close to you
no room between us
seeing a smile
from those ruby lips
inviting for a kiss

taking you in my arms gently
gazing deep in your eyes
the look of love, desire
wanting
needing

the warmth of your body
against the beat of your
kissing gently at first
lips brush each other in passion

thy heart beats faster
senses command
bodies demand
lying on the white sands

the waves lapping at our feet
asking shall we swim my darling
swim in love

it is the magic of love in the moonlight

Peter LeBuhn

Magical Night

a magical night
the moon shines bright
friendships made
friendships resisted...

it was the RED PARTY
a time of gladness
...cheer
...celebration

celebration of the beauty of who we are
GAMES
MUSIC
at the the RED PARTY

Peter LeBuhn

Music Hallfunk

moon has risen
venturing down a dark back alley
the night...misty

far off distance
hearing music
...people playing
...people singing
...people dancing

a music hall
down a cobblestone street
slipping in the side door
the music is overtaking
...into a fierce dancing beat

noticing two ladies by the bar
checking me
playing to them increasingly seductivly

coming upon thee they are
the dream has begun
the fantasy...set in place
the dance we will make
...the future is ours to make
...the future is ours to take

Peter LeBuhn

My Angel

coming into thy life life
on a cool fall eve
finding the door of my heart
beginning to play

beautiful music...i heard
from the start
lightly i heard the pitter-pat of drums
as she talks to me

as the conversation continues
in comes the string quartet
seeing you from afar
beautiful music, my angel, beautiful music

now swooning for you
living for you
love for you
you are my reason
my angel...my angel

Peter LeBuhn

Nature(In All Her Flavor)

nature
(In all her flavor)
silently speaks
though her radiant beauty

she greets each day with a sense of duty
rising over the horizon
the sun slowly awakes
o'er the unfettered waters
singing in each day with new psalters

nature in all her flavor
silent speaks
through her beauty

the white sands
in my toes
the wind in my hair
water running over thy body
it is grand
fresh sea hair

nature
in all her flavor
silently speaks
through her radiant beauty

Peter LeBuhn

Olde Glories...New Promises

the glories of the olde
the promise of the new...things yet to come
what will guide thee
what roads will be taken

thankful for what little has been
keeping the cup watered
for what was once small
will grow in abundance

the glories of the olde
the promise of things yet to come
never to forget
the beginning...the promise made to my country

...my god...my world
to fulfill these glories

into greater promise
olde glories...new promises

Peter LeBuhn

Paris I Adorent

france, her history
her mystery
around each corner
a story is told

the quietness of la seine
the elaborateness of le tour de eiffel
paris i ardent
you are explored
we have developed rapport

en paris ce'st ma couer.
en paris ce'st ma maison.

one day we will meet again
one day we will meet again

Peter LeBuhn

Peter Lebuhn-An Autobiography

peter lebuhn: an autobiography
some say, a simple man
some say, complex
some say full of passion
a gift has been given

a gift has been given
for thee to share with the world
my life
my love
my heart

peter lebuhn is all of these
his words
his actions
speak volumes
as he cares for others

his life is not his own
a gift to to the world
he only aims to please one Master
Jesus Christ

Peter LeBuhn

Pleasure of Thy Heart

love come to be with thee
pleasure of thy heart heart will prove
valleys green
rolling in groves and fields green

shallow waterfalls
sing to thee love songs
doves circle above in approval
golden locks unfurl
rose petals 'neath us

eyes pulling closer
closer...not a word
speaking loudly
with your heart

these pleasures of thy heart
ne'er to depart
pleasures of thy heart
struck by the loving dart

Peter LeBuhn

Puerto Rico

you are in my stocking
hung with care
sights of puerto rico...outside are there

whoooooosing waves
the sea breeze
just you and me
all that matters...you and me

diamonds in your eyes
made you mine
traveling through the ruins of the city
the church...the castles

the museums...paintings of El Greco adorn
living a dream
living a dream
near an island stream

your touch
your love
your tenderness

Peter LeBuhn

Quietness of My Heart

seeing you in the quietness of my heart
presence felt with every beat
your smile...radiance
shines from across the room in radiance

a frenzy of warm happiness
this day we spend together
in the midst of our hearts
our minds...our thoughts...one

in one accord
has entered me at last
at last i am happy

Peter LeBuhn

Serenity

speak to me of serenity
treasures not yet found
peace that flows like a river
not even a sound
tell me of places not yet marred or scarred

visions of standing in the sunlight
against my cheek
as i live, move and breathe
show me paths through the lilies of the field
beds of flowers and buttercups

songs from wrens and meadowlarks are sung.
the lowing of gentle cows
the soft mother cow calls to her colt
lead me past a glass-smooth pond
where frogs croak of coming out parties
graduation from tadpoles to green frogs

find me a peaceful place to sit in the sunlight
thinking quietly
by the pond-side
peace be still
peace be still

copyright 2019

peter lebuhn

written in 25 minutes on a trip to maryland

Peter LeBuhn

Silence

Silence golden in
this moment
through the silence

many thoughts spoken
something happening
strange occurrences
that cannot be unbroken

your smile stretches a mile
bright as the sun
blinding...yet i go nearer
the heart becomes undone
it becomes clearer

you are the one
you are the one

Peter LeBuhn

Sing A New Song

singing to each day a new song
sing a new song
sing out strong
thy life is my song

the gift to be given to everyone
all across the earth
a song for all nations
tribes, tongues

songs of honor and majesty
will be sung
sounds from many lungs
man, woman, child

rejoice, again rejoice
let the heavens be glad and the earth rejoice
let me soar and all that fills it(psalm 96: 11)

the skies will open up
the brightness will blind us
this is the day we meet ourLORD
our savior
our creator

Peter LeBuhn

Slice of Time

sailing through life
on a breeze
entering in
a beautiful woman

stealing part of my life
taking this slice
making it hers
with her pirate smile

heart being stolen
thoughts on the girl
unsure what will unfurl
that slice of time
you own from me

slice of time
precious...
in the right place and the right time
the right woman
the right man

on a breeze
a single second
a slice of time
changes our whole life

Peter LeBuhn

Stand Tall

stand tall
as a mighty tree
undying beauty for all the world to see
storm clouds above

still i see peace
standing tall and strong
nothing fetters
staying strong from the storm

staying strong
our life is a gift
every moment, a treasure
god has given us the ultimate pleasure

Peter LeBuhn

Tapestry of Who We Are

Thy conscious journeys wistfully into the past
responding with passion of life into the present
through this journey the tapestry will be formed and reformed
a mystique, not knowing where the tapestry will go

the past will stay
we will live presently
future is ours to see

as we go we will weave carefully our tapestry of who we are
THE TAPESTRY OF WHO WE ARE

Peter LeBuhn

The Journey Continues

the journey continues
it has been long
staying strong
feeling strong

the journey never ending
it will continue
life will be a tribute

singing a new song
staying strong
the journey has been long
the journey continues

no matter the anger inside the soul
it is gratitude that makes us full of joy.

the journey will remain never ending
it will continue
listening as i go and grow
life will continue as a tribute

Peter LeBuhn

The Living Song

sing a new song everyday
live your song
for the song comes from the soul
you are the song

sing it
sing it

loud like thunder
the seas will part
the heavens will open
in pleasing

sing a new song
sing a new song

the living song

Peter LeBuhn

The One That Got Away! The One That Stayed

lived a life of lost loves
scars across my body
from each woman who has poisoned me
still...my love for the fairer sex remains

all of you got away
in search of love i say

wait a minute...someone newpeeingacross a smoke filled room
the glimpse of you in the alley

you stop...looking at me
with your big brown eyes
the message is clear
in your hesitation
you are the one that will stay

Peter LeBuhn

The Open Door

the open door
Many times clouded by our blind spot
we cannot see
the door never closes for it is our way of future opportunity

the rain may fall
we may stall
the door is open

walk through the door
questions are answered
life becomes clear
WHAT IS MY PURPOSE FOR BEING HERE?

Peter LeBuhn

The Spirit Within

the spirit in me meets the spirit in you
saluting the divine in you
saluting the light of GODwithin you

bringing together my body and soul
focusing my divine potential
bowing to the same potential in you

recognizing that within each of us is
a place where DIVINITY dwells
when we are in that place
WE ARE ONE

Peter LeBuhn

The Teacher

are you the teacher?
the question is asked
...yes...yes is the response
a cold wind blows

a bus suddenly pulls forward
what is about to happen
...life changing off
the bus approaches
the son

the teacher, the father responds
arms open wide
my SON
you have come home
where you belong
next to the fathers side

Peter LeBuhn

The Vessel

put on earth as a vessel
used for HIS will
every move that is made
will determine the future
how our time will be filled

Thy WORD to be preached
in the way of our lives
our talents we grow

without the utterance of your name
people see HIM as you live your life
Through our lives and works
our faith and love is shown for GODabove
our talents from GOD
HOW we use them a gift to HIM

Peter LeBuhn

The Voice on The Radio

your voice on the radio
touches thy heart so
your voice from afar
speaks to thee so dear...so near

smiling and listening
nervously glisten

my name for all the city to hear
is this the beginning
of something dear

Peter LeBuhn

Theatre of The Unknown

seeing you out of the corner of my eye
gnashing your teeth
looking halfway shy
i know i saw you before

can't place where
maybe in that bar
or that night under the stars
are you following me

should i speak
peering at thee
making not a peep
only can i see your thoughts

the smoke clears
you disappear
once again
this hs been
THEATRE OF THE UNKNOWN

Peter LeBuhn

Thedance

in the hills of green
the sunshines asheen
like a panther...you come upon thee
without a warning...a trace

like a panther...coming upon thee
without a warning...a traced
entrance by your charms
you are like royalty
humbly wearing your arms

words are not spoken
understood
the dance has begun
the future is love

Peter LeBuhn

These Dreams

dreams of these
so beautiful
so true

delighting in a horse and carriage ride
winter day in the city, we ride
the boulevard gusting with wind.
the trees dance around

these dreams of these
so beautiful
so true

sauntering along the city sidewalks
talking and laughing
sometimes just the gift of each other
just knowing each other is there

these dreams of these
so beautiful
so true

candlelight dinners
sitting by fireside

these dreams of these
so beautiful
so true

Peter LeBuhn

To The White Sea

the journey is made
being drawn nearer
choices are clearer

feet sinking in the white sands
moon and the stars
shining down
volumes speak in the quietness of thy heart
the roar of the sea
opens up my mind

what stylist? what genius?
painted a land
such as this
alone in the land of thy maker

humbled
feeling small
in awe
of this gift HE has given
most of all

Peter LeBuhn

Transition

transition of love

...transition
...expedition
...relation
...elation
passion into action
...a flavor
...to savor

you and i i and you
love abounds

the two are one
...future yet to become
...becoming one
...the two are one

Peter LeBuhn

What is Love

the question is asked
what is love
bewildered they look
looking around

not a sound
not a shutter
nor a flutter
what is love again asked

love is patient
love is kind
love offers peace of mind

patience is someones ability
to endure through a long trial
what is kindness
kindness is the quality of being generous, considerate, gentleness, warmth and
concern
being kind requires courage and strength

what is peace
peace is freedom from disturbance
peace is tranquility and calmness

that is love

Peter LeBuhn

When Night Becomes Day

when night becomes day
when darkness turns to light
cold wind concedes to the warmth
the passion...heat...affection
RISES

when night becomes day
two worlds collide
a soirée of émotion

when night becomes day
coolness of the night
warmth of the day
under a moonlit night
everything to confide

no divide from deep inside
now day...the warmth of the sun
two worlds collide
when night becomes day

Peter LeBuhn

Without Word

without word
you left for a far off land
...without a plan...you left...i waited and cried for you
what were you going to do?

when the news hit the front page
...thy heart shipwrecked...to the bottom of the sea

without word
you left for a far off land
...without a plan...you left...i waited and cried for you
what were you going to do?

searching the world over
finding no trace
...honey where are you hiding your beautiful face?
i will make you the center of my world
and maybe be happy for awhile

wherever you are in that far off land
...i am with you
...i am with you
we will meet again
i know we will meet again

Peter LeBuhn

Wondouros Life

leading a wondrous life
my heart bleeds love
...my life i give thee
...my love igive to thee

thy garden of fruitful mastery
you enter
all with splender

taking me by the hand
around each corner
...a new surprise
...to find

what a wondrous life i lead
my heart bleeds love

Peter LeBuhn

Printed in the United States
By Bookmasters